SPIRIT

OF

TRUTH

VS.

RELIGION

To Sis Opal
May the Lord bless and
prosper you in 2009.

Rev. Freddie Stuck

SPIRIT

OF

TRUTH

VS.

RELIGION

REV. FREDDIE L. STUCK

Tate Publishing & *Enterprises*

Published by Tate Publishing & Enterprises, LLC
127 E. Trade Center Terrace | Mustang, Oklahoma 73064 USA
1.888.361.9473 | www.tatepublishing.com

Tate Publishing is committed to excellence in the publishing industry. The company reflects the philosophy established by the founders, based on Psalm 68:11,
"The Lord gave the word and great was the company of those who published it."

Book design copyright © 2008 by Tate Publishing, LLC. All rights reserved.
Cover design by Joey Garrett
Interior design by Nathan Harmony

Published in the United States of America

ISBN: 978-1-60696-277-0
1. Biblical Studies: General Studies: General
2. Christian Living: Practical Life: Personal Growth
08.08.19

DEDICATION

I dedicate this book in loving memory of my beloved Mother and Father, whom both have now passed and are with the Lord. They were very loving parents who always encouraged me to be all that I should. My Mother Caroline was always wrapping her arms of love around me and teaching me to care and love others. She also was a wonderful cook. My Dad Charles was a very gentle, loving Dad. He also was a wonderful provider and taught me much in carpentry and woodworking. I couldn't have asked for more loving parents than mine were.

I miss them both very, very much! But I have great peace in my heart, because I know where they are. God Bless you Mom and Dad.

Yours Eternally
Love Freddie L. Stuck, Author

ACKNOWLEDGEMENT

It has been said that an author's mind and heart is like a magician's hat—you cannot take out what was not first put in.

With such consideration, I acknowledge my debt to the following: Carla Eversole, a dear sister in Christ, who has encouraged me and labored alongside me in writing this book. Also my dear beloved Sandra Woolley, who is soon to become my loving wife. She also has supported and encouraged me all the way. Both Sandra, and Carla, have been a great blessing and asset. May the Lord reward and richly bless them both.

In His Love
Rev. Freddie L. Stuck

CONTENTS

The Deception **13**

    A. Doctrines of Men 15

    B. False Spirits and Teachers 17

    C. Religious Spirits 20

    D. Worldly Influence 25

The Falling Away **29**

    A. Battle of The Human Spirit And Soul 30

    B. Carnal Christians. 35

    C. Walking In the Spirit 38

The Love And Pride Of Life **43**

    A. Time for God 46

    B. Repenting In Their Heart 50

    C. Renewing the Mind .52

Repairing the Breach **57**

    A. Right and Wrong Fasting 58

    B. The Only True religion 60

    C. Restoring the Truth. 62

Humility the Key To Restoration **65**

    A. Returning To First Love 67

    B. Preparation for revival 70

    C. The Victorious Church 72

    D. Eternal Joy and Service 73

Confessions for Overcomers. **77**

Christian Leaders On Eternal Rewards **81**

INTRODUCTION

Dear Reader,

I write this book for the instruction and edification of the body of Christ.

I do this by permission and anointing of the Holy Spirit.

This book is not written to judge or damage any of God's children. I write in love and hope that it will help many to understand the difference between religion and truth.

We are in the last days and hours, and I truly believe the Lord Jesus desires that His children become one. Denominations and religions were never God's design and plan for His children. He has always desired that His children walk in truth and love (III John 1:4).

My prayer for each person who reads this book is

that their eyes and heart be opened to the pleading of the precious Holy Spirit.

And that great peace and understanding shall come to them.

Amen!

With Love and Joy

Yours in *Christ Jesus,* Rev. Freddie L. Stuck, Author

THE DECEPTION

Now the spirit speak expressly, that in the Latter
Times some shall depart from the faith, giving
heed to Seducing spirits and doctrines of devils;

Speaking lies in hypocrisy having their
conscience seared with a hot iron;

Forbidding to marry, and commanding to
abstain from meats, which GOD hath created
to be received with thanksgiving of them which
believe and know the truth.

(I Tim. 4: 1–3)

The apostle Paul wrote of this time in which we are now
living. The churches of our times are departing from the
faith and true word of God! Many are allowing different movements and strange doctrines to be taught from
their pulpits. The child of God today watches programs

on television that would cause early Christians to fall to their knees and pray for hours. And marriage is soon becoming a thing of the past.

Brothers and sisters, I speak this shame to myself as well as I write this book. If you would take a look at the two words of verse three in I Tim. 4:3: "believe" and "know" the truth. We, as beloved children of God, believe and know the truth if we truly have been born of God. Amen!

And the word of God also says that truth shall set you free! Free from what? You ask? I'm glad you did.

Free from doctrines of men; free from doctrines of devils, meaning lying spirits. These spirits and doctrines come today through many different channels and ways. Just to speak of a few: cults, religions, false teachers, news, media, religious friends, psychics, etc. Today many are seeking answers to spiritual questions they are deeply concerned about. The only trouble is that they are going to all the wrong people and places for their answers, which is very, very, dangerous. And Satan is waiting to fill their minds and hearts with his lies and deception. And many have very little or no spiritual knowledge of God's Word. How sad that is. And believe it or not, many of these people are God's children who have been born again and should know better.

But the spirits in these false teachers are very alluring and magnetic. They prey on weak Christians who are very carnal in nature. I will speak more later on the carnal Christian in later chapters.

(A) DOCTRINES OF MEN

Have you ever heard anyone say, "That is your interpretation of that scripture." I'm sure you have, if you have witnessed to many of the lost or religious. That is an excuse and reason they believe for running from the spirit of truth. Sorry, but that is the truth. When a true child of God or servant, whichever you choose, speaks the exact scripture chapter and verse in love to a person's spirit (*human*) it will bring great conviction, which in turn will cause that individual to either run away or run to God, depending on how receptive their heart is at that moment. If the Holy Spirit has been dealing with that person's heart concerning those very issues, they generally will yield to his pleading and repent, which means having a change of heart concerning their ways and actions, and bringing them to a decision to follow God and live for Him.

But again, if this person has not received much true

teaching in God's word, they generally will fall away, not allowing the word of God to ground and settle them (II Tim. 2:15). How sad it is that many in these religions and churches today will not allow the truth from the Holy Spirit to teach and guide them (II Tim. 3). My brothers and sisters I plead with you to open your hearts and minds as you read this book. The Lord has prompted me to write this to the true and living body of Christ in love and warning. It isn't easy as you might think, but I must obey the Spirit of God. There are many talk shows on television today which are teaching anything and everything through religion and false doctrine . These are all signs of the end of the church age or age of grace. Please listen to the Holy Spirit. He is warning the Church (*true believers*) to come together in unity of the Word and Spirit of Truth. Jesus said: "My words, they are spirit and they are life to all who receive them," (John 14:16–17).

Many churches today have missed the true message of the Gospel (*Good News*), most teach and place great burdens on their congregation such as certain ways to dress, wear their hair, etc. You get my point! They are men's doctrines not God's (II Tim. 3:16). Many are teaching these ways and ideas and trying to lead many astray, because they believe they have a new revelation from God (Titus 1:7–14). Brothers and sisters, God's Word remains the same! There is only one true revelation, and that was given to the Apostle John on the isle of Patmos. He told John to write to seven churches, which were in Asia. These churches had similar conditions as the churches of today. Ephesus left thy first love; Smyrna rich and blasphemous; Pergamos teaching false doctrine of Balsam; Thyatira allowed false teachings and seducing spirits from a prophetess Jezebel; Sardis works not perfect before God; Philadelphia weak, but has little strength, and has not denied the name of the Lord; Laodiceans Works neither hot nor cold, lukewarm condition, and that is definitely the condition of a lot of the churches today.

(B.) FALSE SPIRITS AND TEACHERS

We are in a very dangerous and troubled time my precious brothers and sisters. We must be alert and vigilant, because Satan, our adversary, is walking around as a roaring lion seeking whom he may deceive and devour. Many today are falling into his snares and traps. And the really sad thing is that some want to. In Matt. 24, the disciples of Christ came to Him as He sat on the mount of Olives and asked this question, "What is the sign of thy coming and the end of the world?" People still are asking the same question. And Jesus is still answering the same way.

First of all let me say this. The world will never actually end as a lot of people think. Again, because of pictures and false teachings many believe the world one day will exist no more. In Matt. 24 Jesus is actually talking about the end of the church age and He is warning His disciples of false teachers and false Christ's. These were the men that Jesus was entrusting the Word of God to spread to the world. But He had to speak to them in parables so that they could be understood in their time of dispensation. Remember they hadn't as yet received the Holy Spirit, who would lead them into all truth! Amen!

And that my Father can send you another comforter! (*The Holy Spirit!*)

Greek (Parakletos) one called along side to help and teach! If you would go next door to the 23rd chapter of Matthew here you see the *Lord* warning all the religious people of his time (Pharisees, Hypocrites, Scribes, and Sadducees). Jesus called all of these religious people blind guides, straining at gnats, and swallowing camels, which make their disciples twofold more the children of hell. Now I don't know about you, but I believe that Jesus was expressing very strongly about how He felt about a person who is a religious hypocrite, and makes others become like that. These people had a form of Godliness but were denying the very power. And the word of God teaches us to turn away from such people, for the very reason that you will become like them. Like I was saying earlier, there are those today who are placing the same burdens on people today! When I began to hunger for the truth of God's Word as a young person, I had no understanding, but the spirit of God was stirring in my heart. I had questions like most everyone else. Why am I here? What is my purpose? And where am I going? But I never questioned, is there a God?

Anybody with common sense knows there is a much greater being who brought this all about. My hunger caused me to search for the true and living God. Even at an early age, I believed He existed. I believe His hand has been on me even before birth.

And I also believe this of everyone. But, sadly, many dismiss this as their own imagination. I was born in the flesh on January 4, 1948, but the second birth (spiritual) didn't come until May 3, 1973. Everyone has an appointed time to receive Christ and also an appointed time to be with the Lord. But if you do not make that appointed time in your heart to receive Him, you will miss the time to be with Him. And that is a true fact brothers and sisters. And I said that for you to understand that these false spirits are doing the devil's will to lead you astray from the truth.

(C) RELIGIOUS SPIRITS

Let me start by saying this. Most people on a whole do not even know of these spirits! First of all let me say religion is a spirit and not the Holy Spirit! Does that shock you? I hope so, for that is the main purpose of the writing of this book. To awake the sleeping church.

I am now talking about the real Body of Christ! The bride if you will (Rev.18:6–9). Let me say at this time there are two symbols mentioned in the book of revelation of two women arrayed in fine clothing. One is a symbol of the bride of Christ, the true church (Rev. 18:6–9). The other is the false or apostate church, and of the antichrist, (Rev. 17:3–6). These two have always been since the day of Pentecost. But when Jesus returns at the second coming, He will at that time destroy this false worldly system, also known as Babylon.

Satan always imitates holy things of God but only to bring death, loss, and destruction (John 10:10).

On the other side, God brings life, peace, joy, and all goodness. This battle has always been about light vs. darkness (John 10:10).

Satan is a thief and a liar. God is love and truth (I John 4:8).

Now let's talk about these religious spirits. They proceed from Satan, not God. These spirits suggest things to the minds of people in a way to make it seem alright and expectable of God. A lot of these spirits are lying spirits, who are able to deceive those who are not educated in God's Word and will accept them as truths. Let me make a point here! These individuals are not possessed of demon spirits. Satan cannot possess any human being unless he is invited. God forbid! But there are those who do worship him and are inviting many spirits to enter.

Now let me talk about these unclean spirits. These spirits promote unclean feelings and thoughts such as porn, sexual assault, and just about every appetite of the flesh. We live in evil times. You can turn on the nightly news and hear of a child being molested, a woman being raped, or someone committing murder. And all this is increasing everyday! Why? Because of these spirits I am talking about.

These spirits also will cause insanity. But remember, like I said, these spirits cannot just take a person over.

If you were to investigate these peoples lives to their past, you would discover times and events where they messed with things of the spirit world, or they themselves were abused and treated wrongly. So you probably have a question like this: Is Satan behind everything wrong? I would have to say *no*! But don't misunderstand me, I am not upholding him, for he is all evil. He will get his influence in if at all possible. Some things start out small and seemingly innocent like I said earlier but become devastating because of the influence of these spirits. It seems we are so quick to prescribe a drug for a problem when it actually could be a spiritual problem. This is where I must say the Church (*body of Christ)* is failing. We are not sensitive to what is going on around us. Most believers in a lot of these denominational churches today have very little concept of spiritual matters. Many are not aware of the power and anointing that the Holy Spirit wants to impart unto them. And then there are those who have been taught that these anointings are not for us, the believers today. How sad! That's exactly what Satan wants, a church without power. But be not discouraged, the Holy Spirit will soon be coming upon all flesh like the Church has never known. So get ready my dear brothers and sisters; real revival is coming soon.

Many churches are growing in size but lack anointing and power, which proceed from the Holy Spirit (Acts 1:8)! Why do the churches fight so much with each other over spiritual gifts? In Matt. 3:10–12, John the Baptist spoke of one who was coming after him who would baptize believers with the Holy Ghost and Fire!

Now brothers and sisters, the Lord did not call me to argue with anyone, but that passage of scripture says exactly what it means and means exactly what it says.

Also, in Mark 16:14–20 Jesus was upbraiding the disciples because of the unbelief and hardness of their hearts. And he spoke of the signs that would follow them as they ministered to others.

How many Christians, or should I say believers, have you seen lay hands on the sick and hurting world?

That's what I thought, not much. And not in a lot of churches. Now I did not say all churches. But as a whole, very little.

(Why?)

Many reasons: fear, lack of anointing, lack of faith,

and many just plain don't believe that's of God. Isn't that also sad?

If you are a believer, you qualify to minister by faith the anointing of healing and deliverance.

Remember, you are a vessel of God for Him to flow through. You are not the healer or baptizer Jesus is.

The word of God also says that the prayer of faith shall save the sick. This means healing of physical and mental conditions, as well as forgiveness of sins. Amen!

Like I said, if the body of Christ was ministering for Jesus the Master, many, and probably in time all, of these problems and attacks of Satan would fail. But for this to happen, Eph. 4:8–16 would have to be in place. I hope as a believer you will read and understand this passage of scripture. Again, the purpose of this book is to open the eyes and hearts of many. That is my prayer!

Can you imagine if every believer on the earth walked in love and unity of the spirit, which means they would be obedient to the leading of the Lord.

Many would be healed, homes and marriages saved, lives changed, and I believe the Lord would return.

But remember, all biblical prophecy must be fulfilled before He does, which means all, even the passages that speak of wars and destruction, because God has everything planned and timed exactly as He chooses.

That doesn't mean that the church should be slothful in service. The enemy is now, and has been for a long time, using his best weapon to allure many away from the truth and God. And that weapon is religion.

(D) WORLDLY INFLUENCE:

As I write this portion of this chapter, please do not misunderstand my meaning. I am not saying that we should not enjoy life, but I am saying that we have let the pleasures of life lead us astray of what God intended. Jesus said, "Take heed to yourselves least at any time your hearts be overcharged with surfeiting, and drunkenness, and cares of this life," (Luke 21:34).

The word ("*surfeiting*") excessive indulgence, ("*as in food or drink*") or simply over indulging!

Many today drink and eat until their bodies are content. God wants us to use moderation in these matters.

There are a lot of Christians who believe it is alright to drink wine or others drinks to be social.

Which is where today, we get the term social drinker. Meaning I don't drink a lot, but just to be sociable. Prov.

20:1 says wine is a mocker, and strong drink is raging, and he that is deceived there by is unwise!

Now another source of worldly influence is to become conformed to this world (Rom. 12:2).

The word conformed means, make or be like, or obey. So you can see that Jesus is warning us not to pattern our lives after the world. And there are several others scriptures to confirm this matter, (Gal. 6:14, II Tim. 2:4, Heb. 11:24, I John 2:15). Many today, believers and non believers, are having trouble with the over indulgence of food. Obesity has now become a plague, not only in the U.S., but worldwide. Brothers and sisters, I am not judging anyone here but just stating a fact. I am also a little over weight, which is not good for our health. So you see, God is warning us not just because it can be sinful, but also dangerous to our health and well being!

Reference scriptures: Amos 6:4, Luke 16:19, Prov. 23:1–2, Prov. 23:21, Phil. 3:18–19, Eccl. 6:7, Is. 56:12.

Now I would like to talk about the pleasures of life. Again it is not sin to have pleasures in life when they are brought of God and also in control. The pleasures I am referring to being wrong are worldly pleasures! Such as greed (Luke 12:19) and lust (I Tim. 5:6, Rom.13:14, Col. 3:5, I Pet. 2:11).

Have you ever heard this worldly term, *"If it feels good, do it,"* or *"Love the one you are with,"* meaning if you can't be with the one you love, *husband* or *wife,* love the one you are with.

Now that is so wrong! Ignorance gone to seed. Sorry but that's the truth. There is no intelligence in those statements.

Faithfulness in marriage today has fallen away because of pornography, television, and books on every sexual imagination you can imagine. To the point now that many in the world except child porn as normal! God help us! Even Catholic priest have been caught and revealed of this horrible sin! In II Tim. 3:13 the apostle Paul said, "That evil men and seducers shall wax worse and worse, deceiving, and being deceived. In second Tim. it says, "This know also, that in the last days perilous times shall come." Notice those two terms. Are we not there? You would have to be totally spiritually and physically blind not to see this.

But many are not paying any attention to this, and that is why many will not be ready for the Lord's return (Matt.24:43–44).

Brothers and sisters be ready, for in the hour you thinketh not, your Lord Jesus will come! Amen!(Matt. 24:44)

There are also many other so-called lifestyles people are trying to introduce into society, such as homosexuality and marriage to more than one wife, known as polygamy!

These churches have formed in our country and are accepting this as holy and right. As it were in the days of Noah, so shall it be in the days of the coming of the son of man!

Jesus our Lord and Savior!

The world was in the same condition then as it is of right now. Also the conditions of Sodom and Gomorrah (Gen 19:24–25, Gen 6:11–13).

THE FALLING AWAY

In the first chapter we talked about the conditions of the world and the churches of our time, which now brings us to the result of these conditions.

Which is a great falling away from that which is Holy and Right before God.

The Apostle Paul speaking to the Thessalonians said:

Let no man deceive you by any means: For that day shall not come except there come a falling away first, and that man of sin be revealed, the son of perdition: Who opposeth and exalteth himself above all that is called God, or that is worshipped; so that he as God sitteth in the temple of God, shewing himself that he is God. This is the Anti Christ the man of sin. Even him, whose all power and signs and lying wonders,

and with all deceivableness of unrighteousness
in them that perish; because they received not
the love of the truth, that they might be saved.

II Thess. 2:3–4

We are in such times and conditions right now. I believe
that man is alive at this very time and is soon to be revealed.
But remember, the Church (true believers) must be taken
out of the earth before this man will be revealed.

And he will bring great power, signs, and lying wonders given to him by Satan! Why? To get all who are here
to believe he is God. I believe this to be the Great Lie.

Many again will believe this man is God, because
their hearts and minds will be blinded.

(A) BATTLE OF HUMAN SPIRIT AND SOUL

I would like to start here by saying that a lot of Christians
lack understanding about the difference between the spirit
and soul of man. I would like to bring more understanding
here by using the Greek words and meanings of them.

Spirit (Gr. Pneuma) wind, breath, also the spiritual
immortal part in man.

The other part of man soul (Gr. psuche) refers to the

animal soul, or life of man, or emotion, will and intellect of man. His mind as we call it.

Now the third part of man body (Gr. Soma) meaning flesh, earthly, house. A place for the spirit and soul of man to live in.

That's why Satan is living illegally here on Earth; he doesn't possess a physical body by physical birth.

I said all that to give you a little better understanding before we explain more in detail.

There is a great battle over the human spirit and soul of man between God and Satan. And that is why God sent His son Jesus, in the flesh, to redeem man from his fall in the Garden of Eden.

You can read of this account in the first chapter of Gen. At this time I must say God speaks to the human spirit of man, where Satan speaks to the human soul of man, and always lies about God and his creation. And that is the very reason Adam fell, because he listened to the lies that Satan spoke to him and Eve.

Satan, like I said, is here illegal, because he had no body (Soma).

Therefore, he entered the body of a serpent illegally, or in other words, overtook it. If you remember in (Gen 1), I said that Satan cannot enter man by force. He has to be invited. In Matt. 4 Satan lied to Jesus by tempting him with hunger. He said if thou be the Son of God, command that these stones be made bread. Jesus answered, "It is written, man shall not live by bread alone, but by every word that proceeded out of the mouth of God."

The next lie he told Jesus was to throw himself down from a high pinnacle or cliff and that the angels of God would bear him up. And many more lies, and they were become lies, because he was trying to get Jesus to tempt God. But the Lord's answer was always, "It is written!" Jesus quoted His Father's word back to Satan.

Finally Jesus said to Satan, "Get Thee Behind Me!" Let me paraphrase that term for today's language: "*Get Out Of My Face!*" Amen!

That is the exact way Adam should have handled the situation in the garden. He did not, but rather listened to Satan. But thank God we have been redeemed by Jesus, the last Adam, through His shed blood on the cross.

God does not want us to be lead by our minds and thoughts alone.

God speaks to our heart or should I say spirit. The center core of our being. And in turn our spirit will bring God's truths up to our minds. And by reading and studying His word, He will apply this to our understanding.

Satan, on the other hand, will lie to your mind to try and get you to believe his lies.

Eph. 6:12 says "For we wrestle not against flesh and blood, but against principalities, against powers, against the rulers of the darkness of this world, against (*Spiritual Wickedness In High Places*)."

Brothers and sisters, we are victorious in Christ Jesus! Let us walk in His Spirit, and we will not fulfill the lust of the flesh. God will always lead you and I in the truth of His precious word.

Brothers and sisters there is a spiritual world which is just as real as this natural world, matter of fact even more real. For, through that world, God spoke this world into existence. Amen!

Unsaved people of this world walk by their minds and bodies, simply because they know no other way.

But the born again child of God learns to walk after the spirit and the Word of God. And the Holy Spirit of God dwells within the believer and will lead him in all truth, if he the believer will allow him.

In the next segment, The Carnal Christian, I will attempt to explain the difference between the Spiritual Christian and the Carnal Christian.

There is a big difference. But for now let us discuss the Spiritual Christian.

What does it mean to walk in the Spirit? In Rom. 8:1 it says, "There is therefore now no condemnation to them which are in Christ Jesus, who walk not after the flesh, but after the Spirit." The word for condemnation in the Greek is (katakrino), which means to pronounce sentence against, deliver for punishment.

In Rom. 8:2 it speaks of the two spiritual laws which are in affect in life: The law of the Spirit of life in Christ Jesus, and the law of sin and death. The law of the Spirit of life in Christ Jesus makes us free from the law of sin and death. The law of the Spirit of life is the wonderful grace of God, through Jesus, His son, who was perfect. And through His sacrifice and shedding of His innocent blood, He once and forever satisfied God the Father forever!

This sacrifice condemned sin in the flesh by triumphing over it and thus fulfilling the law of righteousness for an eternity. The spirit mind is strong because of the holy word of God coming forth into it from God. And it therefore will obey the commands of the Spirit in the love of God. For they that are after the flesh do mind the things of the flesh, but they that are after the Spirit, the things of the Spirit (Rom. 8:5–6).

For to be carnally minded is death, but to be spiritually minded is life and peace! So then they that are in the flesh cannot please God. Now the mind or soul of man has to be changed by the power of the word of God. "The mind that has not been transformed by the word of God, will continue to fight against the Spirit," (Rom. 12:2).

The term born again is the regeneration of the human spirit by the power of the Holy Spirit. And the precious blood of Jesus washes and regenerates the human spirit and is sealed until the day of redemption of the body.

As for understanding any of this process in detail, will only come when we are with Him Gal. 3:13, II Cor. 5:17–21, II Cor. 4:6–10, I Cor. 2:5–12, I Co. 2:14–16, I Thess. 4:13–18.

"And the very God of peace will sanctify you wholly, and preserve you until His coming," (I Thess. 5:23). And now let us move on to the next segment of this chapter. The Lord Bless the reader!

(B) CARNAL CHRISTIANS

Now brothers and sisters in Christ, this is a very touchy subject, but it must be covered.

The Lord Jesus bless his Holy Word to our hearts as

we proceed. Amen! Let us begin by defining the word Carnal (Gr. SARX, flesh) having the nature of flesh, no control of animal appetites governed by mere human nature and not by the Spirit of God (Rom.7–14)! This is the earthly nature of man apart from the divine influence of God, and therefore prone to sin. As you can see, this nature is completely alienated from God. And God will not condone it ever, at anytime. Now for a hard truth: there are many in all the different denominations and religions who have this very nature, and are unsaved, and away from God. But the worse truth is that they don't even realize it because of a lack of knowledge of God's true infallible Word.

Hos. 4:6, which I quote: "My people are destroyed for lack of knowledge: because thou hast rejected knowledge, I also will reject thee, that thou hast forgotten the law of thy God, I will also forget thy children." Here we see a strong warning of the Lord against living in such a state and professing to know Him.

Notice the very first two words in this passage: *my people*. God's talking to all who profess His name and have received the new birth in His Word and are supposed to be walking as new creatures in Christ (II Cor. 5:15–21).

And now you may ask, what denotes a carnal nature? Here are just a few conditions of the carnal nature:

Attends church but does not apply the Word of God to their life, lacks prayer life, does not read God's Word daily, has a critical spirit, and will not witness for Christ publicly. Jesus said, "If you will not confess me publicly before men I will in no wise confess you before my Father."

In Rom. 1–16, the Apostle Paul said, "For I am not ashamed of the gospel of Christ: for it is the power of God unto salvation to everyone one that believeth; to the Jew first and also to the Greek." The word of God also says in Isaiah 54:4 "Fear not: for thou shall not be ashamed: neither be thou confounded; for thou shalt not be put to shame: For tho shalt forget the shame of thy youth, and shalt not remember the reproach of thy widowhood any more."

Here the Lord is talking about *the church* who had strayed from His leading and anointing. And in verse 7–8, He has mercy on them and brings restoration.

My dear brothers and sisters fear is not of God (II Tim 1:7). But fear will keep you from being an effective witness for the Lord. Many are afraid to witness for lack of knowledge of God's Word, but we can change that by studying and spending more time in His Word (II Tim

2:15). And there are those who are afraid of what people might say or do to them.

If you are truly born again, you will have a burning desire to reach the lost. If you do not have a strong desire to tell others about Christ, you might want to examine yourself to see if you really are born of God and in the faith.

Notice here I did not say religious or religion, which has absolutely nothing to do with salvation.

The early church, which is still the same church today, preached nothing but Jesus crucified, buried, and resurrected (I Cor. 1:18). "For the preaching of the cross is to them that perish foolishness, but unto us which are the saved, it is the power of God."

(C) WALKING IN THE SPIRIT

Let me start this out by defining the difference between the two words Spirit and spirit.

Notice that in Romans chapter eight these two words at certain passages are different. One is capitalized, and the other is lower case.

There is a reason for this, The word Spirit, capitalized, means the *Holy Spirit*, whereas the word (*spirit*), lower case, means human spirit. Verse sixteen bears this out: "The Spirit itself beareth witness with our spirit, that we are the children of God."

In the new birth the Holy Spirit takes residence in our spirit, and therefore we are born of God, because He is living inside of every believer that is truly born again.

But if you have not received Jesus by faith into your heart or spirit, you are none of His or not His child if you will. There are those who will try to tell you we are all God's children. But that is not what the Word of God teaches. That is the very purpose of this book, to prove scripturally the truth from God's Word.

Religion does not save anyone from sin, never could, never will.

The world says never say never. But I am telling you the truth from His Word. Now you can believe what you want, that's your choice. But as for me, I will take God's Word over man's. Amen! John 6:63–69 says, "The Holy Spirit quickeneth the Word of God to our human spirit and brings truth and life!"

Before a person is born again of God's Word, they are merely walking dead. In other words, they have no spiritual life in them. I am not talking about physical life. When Adam disobeyed God and ate of the tree in the garden the

Lord had forbidden him. God's Holy Spirit left him. And then Adam was limited to his mind and flesh only.

Adam's eyes were not opened like Satan said, but he became spiritually blind instead.

Remember also in God's Word Jesus said in Matt. 15:14, "Let them alone: They be blind leaders of the blind. And if the blind lead the blind, both shall fall into the ditch."

So if you are truly born again, you will walk in the light of His Word.

And they that be in the night or darkness of the world will stumble and fall into Satan's traps and snares.

But we that are born of God, have His word in us, which bringeth forth light. "For as many as are led by the Spirit of God, they are the sons of God," (Rom. 8:14).

Dearly beloved, if we follow after the ways of the world and traditions of men and their doctrines, they will make the Word of God have no effect on us. For we will believe the religious lies over God's Truth (John 18:37–38). Pontius Pilate, a Roman judge, asked Jesus what is truth.

Pilate could not understand the truth, for he did not have the new birth, for Jesus had not gone to the cross as of yet.

But Pilate's wife heard Jesus speak in other occasions and also witness His crucifixion. And she later received

Jesus as her savior. So you see, when the Holy Spirit of God comes into our heart or human spirit, we will have a change of nature.

Also, as we walk in His Spirit, we will have the victory over flesh. But if we walk after the flesh, we will not be able to please God. For the flesh is contrary to the Spirit and will war against it (John 4:23–24).

For the law was given by Moses, but grace and truth came by Jesus Christ (John 3:8). "The wind blew where it listith, and thou hearest the sound there of, but canst not tell whence it cometh, and whither it goeth: so is every one that is born of the Spirit." That's why the new birth is so wonderful and miraculous. Religion and men's doctrines cannot do that for you.

Religion will allow just about anything you can think of, even sin. Man has always tried to cover his sins with his own ways. The Word of God says: "There is a way which seemeth right unto a man, but the ways and end there of are the ways of death," (Prov. 16:25).

So you see that is the best man made Religion can do. I have said this before, I will say it again:

You can be religious and still split hell wide open. What I am saying is that just being religious will put you there.

My dear reader, I plead with you, if you have not

received Jesus into your heart and your life yet, I pray you do so very soon, before it is eternally too late.

Just ask Him with simple faith, confessing that you have sinned and are a sinner. And ask Him, Jesus, to come into your heart, and He will.

Not because I said it but because His Word promises it. He said he would turn none away (Rom. 10:8–11).

THE LOVE AND PRIDE OF LIFE

Here the Apostle Paul is talking about the last days, saying perilous times shall come. The word perilous here means very dangerous. He goes on to express the condition of people of this time:

> For men shall be lovers of their own selves, covetous, boasters, proud, blasphemers, disobedient to parents, unthankful, unholy, Without natural affection, trucebreakers, false accusers, incontinent, fierce, despisers of those that are good, Traitors, heady, highminded, lovers of pleasures more than lovers of God; Having a form of godliness, but denying the power thereof: From such turn away. For of this sort are they who creep into houses, and

lead captive silly women laden with sins, led away with divers lusts, Ever learning, and never able to come to the knowledge of the truth.

2 Tim 3:17

When you read this, it does describe our time. Evil is abounding on every street in our nation. And all of these conditions fit the very nature of a lot of people today.

That's very sad, but if the shoe fits you wear it, so says the world.

But you see, I am no longer of this world, for I have been born of God. Praise His wonderful name.

Pride of life and self out of control are a bad thing. Lucifer, the greatest arch angel God created, fell because of that very reason. Is. 14:12–17 says He was beautiful in appearance, all the colors of the rainbow and then some. But he became so proud that he began to boast of his power and beauty.

He was called son of the morning. "For thou hast said in thine heart, I will ascend into heaven," (verse 13).

I will exalt my throne above the stars of God! I will sit also upon the mount of the congregation, in the sides of the north." What does that sound like to you? Wrong move!

For he was cast out of heaven and fell as lighting.

Other reference scriptures include: Ezek. 28:12–19, Rev. 12:3–17. You see, Satan is the accuser of the brethren but can no longer approach God in heaven (Job 1:6–12). Satan from the earth is still trying to test God through men and their weakness of the flesh. But if you read the whole account of Job, you will see that the Lord restored him twofold of what he had before his temptation. Many are the afflictions of the righteous, but God deliverth them out of them all. Praise His name Amen!

As we have read and studied these passages of scripture, it's very easy to see why people down through the ages are filled with pride and jealously and desire to rule the earth. It comes from their father, the Devil.

Jesus called him the Prince and Power of the air and the God of the earth. Temporary! But he is soon to be judged and placed where he belongs, the lake of fire which burns eternally.

Unfortunately, there will be many others who will also join him in that place of torment, and only because they refused and rejected the precious Son of God.

(A) TIME FOR GOD

This I believe is the most important part of our walk with the Lord.

Many today are far too busy to give God time in their day. Someday they will have no time, for time for them will end, and eternity will begin. You see, we live on this earth in a time, or should I say dispensation of time. This was created by God for the earth. Man made the calendar and time zones. God made the seasons for seed time and harvest, which He said in His word will be always and forever (Eccl. 3:1–14, John1:1–5).

The Apostle Paul in Gal. 4: 1–11 speaks of their fleshly natures after they had received Christ, "but yet they were still living after the weak and beggarly elements, whereunto they still desired to be in bondage. He said unto them, you observe days, and months, and times, and years. And then he said I am afraid of you, lest I have bestowed upon you labor in vain." What he was saying was that he committed the truth of God's Word to them and nurtured them to where they loved Paul so much that they would even have plucked out their eyes for him. But then when you received the truth, I became your enemy.

He, Paul, did not understand why they still desired to be under the law.

He had presented them the Grace of Jesus, and they still desired to be in bondage under the law.

We have many today, who like those Galatians, are under Religious bondage, which is exactly what Paul was talking about. Unless the spirit of God opens the spiritual eyes of men, they will have no spiritual understanding.

I would like to now talk about a promise of God in His Word to all who will believe and accept it (Heb 4: 1–11). I am talking about the rest of God. Our Lord desires that we enter into rest. And by doing so, we will completely trust Him and cease from our own works. The reason for this is that the Lord will be able to entrust things through us that will strengthen and aid others. When we enter this rest we are still free moral agents but led by His precious Spirit and will. We will then be led by His Spirit in a much deeper understanding of His desire for our lives.

(Eph. 3: 16–21). If you will read Eph. 4:1–16 you will get a wonderful understanding of what the Lord wants for each and every child of His.

If the Body of Christ walked in those truths, I believe we would have a much different world than we now have today. But sad to say, again, many do not even care about the things of God. Therefore we have a world proceeding on a course of destruction. And that is why God will soon intervene in the affairs of men. Because if He didn't, man would literally destroy earth and himself through ignorance. And believe me today, ignorance has gone to seed!

Very few in the world even know, or care enough, to read God's inspired Holy Word. The ones that do, love and pray for all. Like I said, except they let the Holy Spirit lead them into all truth though deep humility. They cannot and will not be saved. Jesus said, "I am the way and the truth. No man cometh unto the Father but by me," (John 14:6, John 15:1–17, John 10:1–11, I John 5: 11–13). Here we can see and accept the truth, if we will only open our hearts to God. Many religions teach of good and wonderful things, but they cannot deliver eternal life. The only true way to God the Father is through His only begotten son Jesus.

There is no argument here beloved. His tomb is empty! All other leaders of these worldly religions have not that claim. Their bones and dust are still in the graves or tombs as of this very day.

You would think that I would not have to say any-more concerning that matter right? Wrong! There are many, through ignorance and lack of enlightenment of their spirit, who will argue with you always if you let them. Let me say this to that matter:

> Speak unto the children of Israel, saying, if a soul shall sin through ignorance against any of the commandments of the Lord concerning things which ought not to be done, and shall do against any of them.
>
> (Lev. 4:2)

Also the Apostle Paul in I Cor. 14: 37–38 said, "If any man think himself to be a prophet, or spiritual, let him acknowledge that the things that I write unto you are the commandments of the Lord. But if any man be igno-rant, let him be ignorant." Remember here that the word ignorant means error or going astray and also unlearned of the Word of God.

No need to argue, if one wants to remain ignorant to the truth of God's Word, let him do so. But I would say to those, you must answer to the Lord someday soon and give an account of your life.

For it is appointed once for a man to die, and then

the to be judged of God. I believe there are many appointments in life for each and every one of us. And I also believe that every moment of our lives is appointed of God. Please do not insinuate that I am saying that God is waiting for you to make mistakes and then punish you. No! What I am merely saying is He's watching you in love, and yes He does know every intent of your heart (and I believe even before we do things). That's how great and wonderful He is.

He also watches over the righteous to protect them. Psalm 91 bears that out verily plainly.

(B) REPENTING IN THE HEART

Repentance! What does that mean to you?

Let's start by understanding the meaning of true repentance. To repent actually means to have a change of mind and heart. In a theological and ethical sense, repentance is a fundamental and thorough change in the hearts of men from sin and towards God. Although, faith alone isn't the only condition for salvation (Eph. 2:8–10, Acts 16:31).

Repentance is bound up with faith and inseparable from it. And without some measure of faith, no one can truly repent, and repentance never attains to its deepest character until the sinner realizes through saving faith, how great is the grace of God against who he has sinned.

On the other hand, there can be no saving faith without true repentance.

Repentance contains these essential elements:

1. A genuine sorrow toward God or account of sin (II Cor. 7:9–10, Matt. 5:3, Ps. 51).
2. An inward repugnance to sin, necessarily followed by the actual forsaking of it (Matt. 3:8, Acts 26:20, Heb. 6:1)
3. A humble self-surrender to the will and service of God (Acts 9:6).

Now most people feel a sense of repentance out of fear because of the judgment to come. That's alright, but God would want us to repent with a godly sorrow, for it is truly from the heart, not just because we get caught in the act of sin, what ever it was. For example, Peter showed a godly sorrow, for he wept deeply and repented. An on the other hand, Judas had a worldly sorrow and could not find a place of repentance and hanged himself from a tree in a field called the field of blood (Matt. 27:1–10).

Now to simply repent and truly mean it, you must

confess with your mouth the Lord Jesus, and believe in your heart God raised Him from the dead, and you shall be saved.

For with the heart man believeth unto righteousness, salvation. For the scripture saith, whosoever believeth on Him, shall not be ashamed. Now I do not believe Christianity to be a religion like others do, because Christianity involves a man being sacrificed on a cross and shedding his blood for the remission of our sins and failures. Without the shedding of blood there is no (remission) or removing of sin (Rom.5:6–9, Rom. 5:18, Rom. 6:22–23, Rom. 3:22–26).

(C) RENEWING THE MIND

Now let us explore the subject of renewing the mind. Without a renewed mind, or should I say restored mind, one will not be able to walk in newness of life, which is the new birth (Rom. 10: 8–11). There is such a thing as right and wrong thinking. Especially when it involves living a life that is pleasing and acceptable to God. If you noticed in Rom. 12:2, we are not to be conformed to this world, but be transformed by the renewing of our minds. Why? So that we may be able to prove what is that good, and acceptable, and perfect, will of God. Being a pastor, many people ask you at times what the will of God is. And really it is very simple; His Word is His will. A lot of times, many will say, "I wish I knew what God's will is for me." And I would say to them, read His Word in an attitude of prayer, then be quiet and listen from your heart.

God will speak to your heart with a small, still voice. Yes God can speak audibly but probably not, because He hasn't spoke that way since the Holy Spirit was sent down to man. The Holy Spirit is also referred to as the Spirit of truth. Jesus said, "In that day you shall ask me nothing, but what so ever you ask the Father in my name I will do it."

So you see the proper way to pray is to the Father, asking in the name of Jesus. When Jesus was on earth, he did or said nothing except what the Father revealed to him. And now we also have another comforter. The Holy Spirit!

In the Greek parakletos means one called along side to help. That means he will guide and instruct us in all truth according to what the Father speaks to him (Rom. 8:26–27). You see, right here is where world religion stumbles at the truth of the bible, because the Word of God speaks of a God with three personalities, Father, Son, and Holy Spirit. Many religions do not accept this as a spiritual truth of God's Word. But then they really don't preach the true word of God anyway.

Jehovah Witnesses are one of them.

They base their religion on the visitation of an angel which spoke to an individual of that belief and was said to have given him a new revelation. Folks, that is very dangerous! I would not want to stand before Jehovah God and give an account of false teaching that was not spoken of God. Here is what the Lord says:

> The anger of the Lord will not turn back, Until He has executed and preformed the thoughts of His heart: In the latter days you will understand it perfectly.
>
> But if they had stood in My counsel, And had caused My people to hear My Words, Then they would have turned them from their evil way. And from the evil of their doings.
>
> "I have not sent these prophets, yet they ran. I have not spoken to them, yet they prophesied.
>
> Jer. 23:20–22

This sounds like the very days we are now living in. Amen!

Brothers and sisters, a lot of the teachings today are going astray from the truth of God's Word.

The Spirit of God has moved upon my heart to write this book, and reveal the truth of His Word back into the hearts of all who will receive and understand it. I am not writing this book for profit but for warning. This was given to me from the Holy Spirit through the Father and Jesus to warn His children of His soon return that they might be ready to leave with Him. All that love Him, Jesus, will the Father bring with Him to glory.

REPAIRING THE BREACH

We are now moving into a portion of the Word of God that is going to open the eyes of many I pray.

Let me start off by explaining the meaning of the word breach which is the breaking of a law, breaking of a promise, or breaking of a contract.

But what we are talking about in this scripture is breaking of God's Holy word and Commandments, which a lot of us have gotten away from. The Lord desires to repair this breach, if you will only let Him:

> Cry aloud spare not lift up thy voice like a trumpet, and shew my people their transgression, and the house of Jacob their sins. Yet they seek me daily, and delight to know my ways, as a

nation that did righteousness, and forsook not the ordinance of their God: they ask of me the ordinances of justice; they take delight in approaching to God.

Is. 58: 1–2

Here we see a description of God's people at that time, and the prophet Isaiah was explaining their condition, which God was displeased with. The Lord then goes on to reveal to them the proper fast that He desires. They were fasting for all the wrong reasons.

(A) RIGHT AND WRONG FASTING

In verse 4 of Is. Chapter 58, the Lord said:

Behold ye fast for strife and debate, and to smite with the fist of wickedness; ye shall not fast as ye do this day, to make your voice to be heard on high. Many today are fasting the same way thinking God is hearing their prayers because of their fast.

Isaiah 58:4

All you will accomplish there is a great hunger and no results. Although, if you fast long enough, you just might lose a little weight. Ha, Ha! Sorry I couldn't resist a little laugh there.

Do you see how silly we can be with our own ideas and doctrines?

Now look at verse 5:

> Is it such a fast that I have chosen? A day for a man to afflict his soul? Is it to bow down his head as a bulrush, and to spread sackcloth and ashes under him? Wilt thou call this a fast, and an acceptable day to the Lord?
>
> Isaiah 58:5

Here the Lord is still asking questions of the people of that time and yet also of this very time. All of this is ceremonial and not from the hearts as God desires.

Now the Lord goes on to explain the right fast and for the reasons He chooses:

> Is not this the fast that I have chosen? To loose the bands of wickedness, to undo the heavy burdens, and to let the oppressed go free, and that ye break every yoke?
>
> Is it not to deal thy bread to the hungry, and that thou bring the poor that are cast out to thy

house? When thou seest the naked, that thou cover him; and that thou hide not thyself from thine own flesh.

Isaiah 58:6–7

Now we see the Lord talking about feeding the hungry, and bringing the poor to your house.

How many people are actually doing this today? Also, He talks about not hiding yourself from your own flesh. Here He is talking about your family. Today families are growing apart more and more. I have even seen a lot of this since I was a child in the 1950's. There is very little closeness in many families today.

Now in verse 8 through 14, the Lord explains the good things that will begin to happen in our lives if we honor Him in the right fast and obey Him.

If you read them you will see the breach being repaired as the Lord desires.

(B) THE ONLY TRUE RELIGION

Pure religion and undefiled before God and the Father is this, To visit the fatherless, and widows in their affliction, and to keep himself unspotted from the world," James 1:27.

Now you can see what religion God honors and accepts. And whether you believe it or not, that is the only religion He recognizes.

When Jesus walked the earth, that is exactly what he was doing, healing the sick who were afflicted of all kinds of illnesses. He also cast many spirits out of people.

Look at some of the things people are doing today: murdering innocent people, molesting little children, raping women, and many more things which just stagger our minds. Folks, we are living in the very times and days the bible talks about.

The intensity and increase of these signs are growing rapidly.

We are in those last days the Word of God talks about. Men are lovers of themselves, proud, boasters, unholy, and don't respect human life. Not to speak of how we are trashing out our plant.

If you read the book of Revelation, you will see many conditions which are soon to come. On our currency a phrase is written, *In God We Trust.*

Now I believe our forefathers did, but do we really? And as a nation. *One Nation Under God* indivisible, with liberty and justice for all, says the pledge of allegiance.

Excuse me, but I believe we should all get on our

knees with that lie. If that is a pledge, then don't you believe that we need to honor it before God?

Now at this time, I would like to quote this scripture:

> If my people which are called by my name, shall humble themselves, and pray, and seek my face, and turn from their wicked ways; then will I hear from heaven, and will forgive their sin, and will heal their land.
>
> II Chronicles 7:14

(C) RESTORING THE TRUTH

"Lying lips are abomination to the Lord: But they that deal truly are his delight." (Prov. 12:22)

The truth is so easy for many to get around today. You have heard that it is alright to tell a little white lie once in a while. Wrong!

And the reason for that is that lies beget lies. Lying is an addiction, just like other bad habits. Lying also can bring grave consequences to our lives. And if you make a habit of lying, soon no one will believe a word you are saying.

What I would like to know is, why do we put size and

color on lies? Lies are all black. And there is no size. A lie is a lie before God. Even lying to protect someone is wrong.

Yet a lot of times, we find ourselves doing it.

Rom. 3:4 says, "God forbid: Yes, let God be true, but every man a liar: as it is written, That thou mightiest be justified in thy sayings, and mightiest overcome when thou art judged.

Titus 1:2 says, "When the Lord Jesus returns soon, and rules and reigns. He will do it with a rod of iron."

And that is the truth, His Holy Word. Amen!

Everything at this time, that is right and good and true, will be restored to what God intended in the beginning. This period of time is at the end of the Church age, which is called the thousand year Millennium Reign of Christ.

The word Millennium comes from the Latin word mille, meaning thousand, years, a theological term based upon Rev. 20. At this time, Jesus will establish His kingdom over Israel (Acts 1:6).

So as you can see absolute truth will soon be restored, Amen! Praise the Lord!

HUMILITY THE KEY TO RESTORATION

Now before truth can be restored back into our lives, there must be one main ingredient put back in place of humanity. And that is heart felt humility before God, which in turn will bring a godly sorrow, which will bring true repentance before God. Also Prov. 16:19 says, "Better it is to be of an humble spirit with the lowly, than to divide the spoil with the proud."

Remember Lucifer, Satan, fell because of his pride.

As a matter of fact, that became his very nature, which caused him to be cast out of heaven. And in a big hurry. As lighting if you will. Ha! Ha!

Now look at this scripture in Matt. 18:14, "Whosoever therefore shall humble himself as this little child, the same is greatest in the kingdom of heaven." Luke 18:14 says, "Now we are without excuse of the will of God concerning this matter." Here we read in (Mic. 6:6–8):

> Where with shall I come before the Lord, and bow myself before the high God? Shall I come before him with burnt offerings, with calves of a year old? Will the Lord be pleased with thousands of rams, or with ten thousands of rivers of oil? Shall I give my firstborn for my transgression, the fruit of my body for the sin of my soul?
>
> He hath shewed thee, O man, what is good; and what doth the Lord require of thee, but to do justly, and to love mercy, and to walk humbly with thy God?
>
> Micah 6:6–8

Also in James 4:10: "Humble yourselves in the sight of the Lord, and He shall lift you up. If you notice the Lord is saying to us, humble yourselves." We have to commit our heart in humility before God, before we ever enter His presence.

And today we can come to the throne of grace boldly, but in love and humility, because of the precious blood of Jesus His son, which tore down the wall of partition between us and the Holy Father of God. In the Old Testament, under the Law, men could not approach God except through a high priest, who through washings and rituals, could only be accepted into the Holy of Hollies, which is where the Ark of Covenant was. At that time the Spirit of God would come down into the ark to speak to man. Thank God we don't have to go through all those ceremonies today. Amen!

That was the only way they could approach God, and if any man tried to enter the Most Holy Place without the High Priest, he died instantly. Even the High Priest had to have a rope tied around his right ankle, in case he was not accepted, to be dragged back out. Job 23:15 says, "But now Jesus has washed us from our sins, and made us priests and kings unto God His Father.

(A) RETURNING TO OUR FIRST LOVE

Let me start this segment by asking you a question: Who or should I say, what, would you say is your First Love? You would be very surprised at the answer I would get. I actually did ask certain people at times that very question, just to see what their answers would be. And I was amazed at their answers. Actually I was shocked, because the people that I asked this question were church people. What I mean by that is people who professed to know Jesus as their Savior. Most of them said their husbands or wives were their first loves.

Others said their children was their first love.

You see, when you live your life for God, you see that everything you are and have is because of Him.

Then it's not hard to realize He, Jesus, is your First Love.

This is a hard subject to talk about here, but I must.

Some people do not cope well with loss.

And the greatest loss in life is losing a very close loved one in death. Some cannot accept it, and even lose their minds. And that is exactly why Jesus should be your first love, to bring you comfort through the Spirit in those times.

I said it is a hard subject and it is. I have been accused of being insensitive, but that is not true at all. We all have our ways of grieving over a loss so precious. Some of us may hold in our feelings and emotions better than others. But it doesn't mean we don't feel the hurt and the pain of loss. I just lost both of my dear parents recently. And believe me, it hurts so. But I have the Lord's Word and promises that hold me strong. Amen!

1. John 14:1–4 says, "Let not your heart be troubled: ye believe in God, believe also in me."

2. In my Father's house are many mansions; if it were not so, I would have told you. I go to prepare a place for you.

3. And if I go and prepare a place for you, I will come again, and receive you unto myself; that where I am there ye maybe also.

4. And whither I go ye know, and the way ye know.

Now that comforts me. For in the very first verse, He said let not your heart be troubled. God wants us to know we shall all be with Him in heaven someday, where there will be no more trouble, pain, and death.

Yes that's what I said, no more death. You see death is an enemy. God never intended for anyone to die. The earth would have been replenished anyway without sin and death.

I Cor. 15:55–58 says, "You see the sting of death is gone, which is sin. And now Praise to the Lord Jesus, who has redeemed us from sin and death, unto life everlasting!"

(B) PREPARATION FOR REVIVAL

This segment is about preparing our hearts for the revival that is even now in progress as I speak, (Joel 3:13–14, Joel 2: 23–30, Hos. 10:12). Here the Lord is talking about His people sowing righteousness and mercy and breaking up the follow ground—our indifferences and unbelief. Then, and only then, will the Lord rain righteousness upon us (speaking of the true church, the Body of Christ, if you get my understanding.) Many churches want revival, and so they invite speakers and evangelists in hopes of reviving their church.

When, in truth of the matter, they would revive each other by allowing the Holy Spirit to flood their hearts with His love and joy. Those are the very first two fruits of the Spirit. These fruits are alive inside of believers, and they just need to allow them to flow out on others. Amen!

Many churches are dead and dry, because they will not allow the sweet presence of the Holy Spirit to move in them. Many say, "We don't want no wild fire here." And generally they don't have to worry; they won't probably have any fire.

The Holy fire from the Spirit will indeed burn the worldly dross from our spirits, if we only will allow Him (Acts 1:8, Matt. 3:10–12).

The Holy Spirit is very gentle and will never force himself upon anyone. He must be loved and invited. But would you believe many church people, who are carnal in their walk, do not even know there is a Holy Ghost? That is sad in many ways, and if they are not born again through the blood of Jesus, they will also miss heaven (I Cor. 2:5–16). The Holy Spirit reveals many things to the believer by the gifts of the spirit. These are special anointings given by Jesus (Eph.4:8–16). Most of the denominational churches know nothing of the gifts of the spirit. And, therefore, there will be no teaching in them on that subject. And if any of these church members hear of these gifts and inquire in their churches, they are usually told they are not for us today.

And my question then is: Why would the apostle Paul mention them to the church of Ephesus? Read verse 16 again. There's why!

And now we can begin to see why there is no revival in the churches of today. Amen!

The word revive means to bring back to life or consciousness. Isn't that interesting? Also, here's another word which I find quite similar resuscitate, which means to bring back from apparent death. That's exactly what the Spirit of Truth does, revives or resuscitates the human spirit. You see that's what Rom. 8:6 says: "For to be carnally minded is death; but to be spiritually minded is life and peace."

(C) THE VICTORIOUS CHURCH

When you think of the word victorious, you immediately relate that thought to winning or winner.

And that is exactly what the Lord is saying through the Apostle Paul in Rom. 8: 36–39. Paul says, "Nay, in all these things we are more than conquerors through Him that loved us." He goes on to describe a list of things present, and things to come, and even height nor depth. In others words nothing.

Now that's victorious. Amen!

After all, if God be for us, who can be against us? And what that passage is really meaning is: shall not prevail against us. Now in I Cor. 15:57–58 says:

> But thanks be to God which giveth us the victory through our Lord Jesus Christ.
> Therefore my beloved brethren, be ye steadfast, unmovable, always abounding in the work of the Lord, forasmuch as ye know that your labor is not in vain in the Lord.
>
> I Cor. 15:56–58

Notice Paul did not say abound in religion, but in the work (Phil. 3:9–11, Ps. 26:3).

The Lord bless this unto your hearts. Amen!

(D) ETERNAL JOY AND SERVICE

In this segment I would like to talk about the joy of the Lord, which is our strength.

Neh. 8: 10 says:

> Thou wilt shew me the path of life: in thy presence is fullness of joy; at the right hand there are pleasures for evermore. We cannot even imagine in this life what that fullness of joy is like!
>
> But when we come into His presence, that's when our spirit man rejoices in that fullness. I'm sure you have heard of that term, Joy Unspeakable and Full of Glory. That's exactly what they are talking about when we are in His presence.

And that's where the term slain in the Spirit also comes from. It's an experience when one enters God's Presence and anointing, where the Spirit over whelms them, and many can, and will, lose physical strength to stand. This is also known as the *shekinah* (she-ki-na) of God's Glory.

Here are several scriptures that took place in the old and new testaments or covenants: Ex. 40: 35, Lev. 16: 2, II Sam. 6:2, I Kin. 8:10, II Chr. 5:13, Ps. 80:1, Is. 37:16, Ezek. 9:3, Luke 2:9, Acts 7:55, II Cor. 3:18.

You see God is sovereign and independent and chooses as He wills to move upon man.

And when He does, He will get your undivided attention. God is not in a hurry, but very patient with man, not willing that any should perish, but come to a saving knowledge of the truth. I pray that those that are without Christ through reading this book will come to that saving knowledge and receive Jesus into their hearts by faith. Amen!

The Bible says that we are "laborers together with God," (I Cor. 3: 9). Well, if we work together with God, we will have to be workers of miracles, because He is a miracle working God!

Sin dethroned man from the miracle realm, but through grace He is coming into His own. It has been a hard struggle for us to grasp the principles of this strange life of faith.

Sin has made us workers—grace would make us trusters.

In the beginning, man's spirit was the dominant force in the world; when he sinned, his mind became dominant—sin dethroned the spirit and crowned the intellect; but grace is restoring the spirit to its place of dominion, and when man comes to recognize the dominance of the spirit, he will live in the realm of the supernatural without effort. No longer will faith be a struggle and fight, but an unconscious living in the realm of God.

The spiritual realm is man's normal home; it places him where communion with God is a normal experience where faith in the miraculous, miracle - working God is unconscious, where he will exercise the highest type of faith and yet be as unconscious of having exercised faith as he is when he writes a check.

(Kenneth E. Hagin, *The Name of Jesus)*

The Church's problem has been that we have lived beneath our privileges so long, we think that is normal Christianity. But it is abnormal.

Absolutely abnormal Christianity! The whole Church, the Pentecostal, Full Gospel, charismatic move included, is in a babyhood stage. We're trying to have faith. We're trying to believe.

But, thank God, some are coming to see the light

of God's Word. And I am more convinced today than I was yesterday that in these last days there is going to arise a company of believers who will see and know their authority, their rights, and privileges in Christ. They will know that the name of Jesus belongs to them. They will take up that name and start using it as unconsciously as they take their car keys and unlock the car door, then put them in the ignition and start the car.

God's Word contains God's thoughts. Those thoughts are as high above man's thoughts as heaven is above the earth (Is. 55:8–9).

You have to get the revelation of God's Word in your heart—your spirit. Your natural mind cannot receive the things of the Spirit of God. They are spiritually discerned.

The church will never see these things unless they are taught (God put teachers in the Church to teach) but it will come, little by little. And when it comes in its fullness, and we grow out of the babyhood stage of Christianity, and realize our rights and privileges, and the authority and power in that Name, and rise up to use that Name. It will be said of us as it was of the early disciples, "These that have turned the world upside down are come hither also," (Acts 17:6).

CONFESSION FOR OVERCOMERS

My body is a temple for the Holy Spirit:

1. Redeemed

2. Cleansed

3. Sanctified by the Blood of Jesus

4. My members, the parts of my body, are instruments of righteousness.

5. Yielded to God for His service and for His glory. The devil has no place in me, no power over me, no unsettled claims against me. All has been settled by the blood of Jesus.

6. I overcome Satan by the blood of the Lamb and by the Word of my testimony, and I love not my life unto the death.

7. My body is for the Lord and the Lord is for my body.
8. Praise the Lord! Amen!

1. I Cor. 6:19
2. Eph. 1:7 & Ps. 107:2
3. I John 1:7
4. Heb. 13:12
5. Rom. 6:13
6. Rom. 8:33–34
7. Rev. 12:11
8. (8) I Cor. 6:13

Dear Reader:

I hope you have enjoyed my book *Spirit Of The Truth Vs. Religion*."

As you can see now *religion* is not God's plan or design for your life. God wants His children to overcome in this life and the next life also. He is returning "soon" for a church that is victorious and without spot or wrinkle, or in other words, an overcoming, glorious church. Our God is an overcomer, therefore, so shall His children be. Amen!

Lord! I pray now in the name of Jesus, for all who read this book: That Christ may dwell in your hearts by faith; that ye, being rooted and grounded in love, may be able to comprehend with all saints what is the breath, and length, and depth, and height; and to "know" the love of Christ, which passeth knowledge, that ye might be filled with all the fullness of God.

Now unto Him that is "able" to do exceeding, abundantly above all that we ask or think, according to the power that worketh in us.

Unto Him be glory in the church by Christ Jesus throughout all ages, world without end. Amen!

The Lord bless you richly,
Rev. Freddie L. Stuck

CHRISTIAN LEADERS ON ETERNAL REWARDS

Now when Christ says: Make to yourselves friends, lay up for yourselves treasures, and the like, you see that He means: Do good, and it will follow of itself without your seeking, that you will have friends, find treasures in heaven, and receive a reward.

Martin Luther

God will reward everyone according to His works. But this well consistent with his distributing advantages and opportunities of improvement, according to his own good pleasure.

John Wesley

The primary purpose of the judgment seat of Christ is the examination of the lives and service of believers, and the rewarding of them for what God considers worthy of recognition.

Theodore H. Epp

There will be varying degrees of reward in heaven. That shouldn't surprise us: There are varying degrees of giftedness even here on earth.

John MacArthur Jr.

The believer has his foundation in Jesus Christ. Now we are to build upon this foundation, and the work we have done stand the ultimate test: Final exams come at the judgment seat of Christ when we receive our reward.

Billy Graham